SENDING SECRETS

By M. C. Hall

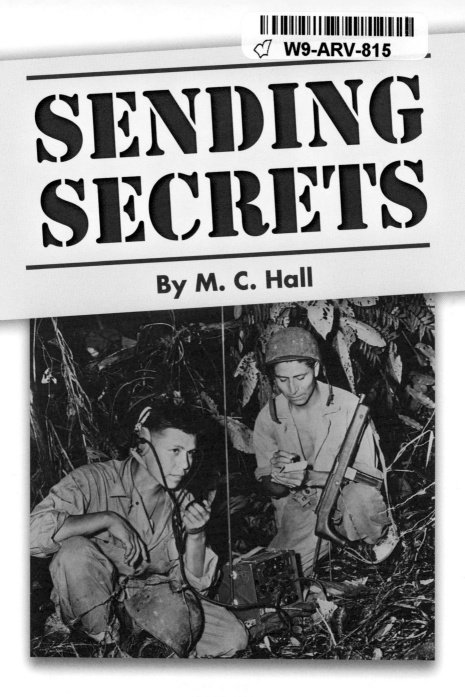

Scott Foresman
is an imprint of

PEARSON

Glenview, Illinois • Boston, Massachusetts • Chandler, Arizona •
Upper Saddle River, New Jersey

Photographs

Every effort has been made to secure permission and provide appropriate credit for photographic material. The publisher deeply regrets any omission and pledges to correct errors called to its attention in subsequent editions.

Unless otherwise acknowledged, all photographs are the property of Pearson Education, Inc.

Photo locators denoted as follows: Top (T), Center (C), Bottom (B), Left (L), Right (R), Background (Bkgd)

Opener: ©Marilyn Angel Wynn/Nativestock; **1** Corbis; **6** Corbis; **7** ©Margaret Bourke-White/Time Life Pictures/Getty Images; **8** ©Marilyn Angel Wynn/Nativestock; **9** National Archives; **10** Corbis; **11** Navajo code radio talkers of 1st US Marine Division, 1944 (b/w photo), American Photographer, (20th century)/Private Collection/©Peter Newark Pictures/Bridgeman Art Library; **12** Corbis.

ISBN 13: 978-0-328-46916-1
ISBN 10:   0-328-46916-5

3 4 5 6 7 8 9 10 V010 13 12 11 10

Can you read this note? It's written in a code! We use codes to send secret messages. Turn the page to see what the message says.

19-20-1-18-20   5-1-3-8

4-1-25 23-9-20-8   1

19-13-9-12-5!

KEY

A =1	J =10	S =19
B =2	K =11	T =20
C=3	L =12	U =21
D =4	M=13	V =22
E =5	N =14	W =23
F =6	O =15	X =24
G =7	P =16	Y =25
H =8	Q =17	Z =26
I =9	R =18	

Codes use one thing to stand for something else. Sometimes letters are mixed up. A key tells you how to read the code. Use the key to read the message.

19-20-1-18-20   5-1-3-8

4-1-25 23-9-20-8   1

19-13-9-12-5!

Start each day with

a smile!

People use codes in war. In 1942, the United States was at war with Japan. Our ships and soldiers were far away. Soldiers needed to send messages to each other. They needed a code to keep the messages a secret.

Some Navajo soldiers came up with a plan. Besides members of the Navajo nation, only a few people in the world could speak the Navajo language. The men made up a code that used Navajo words. These men were called "Code Talkers."

NAMES OF ORGANIZATIONS (Con't)

MILITARY MEANING	NAVAJO PRONUNCIATION	NAVAJO MEANING
Battalion	Tacheene	Red Soil
Company	Nakia	Mexican
Platoon	Has-clish-nih	Mud
Section	Yo-ih	Beads
Squad	Debeh-li-zini	Black Sheep

COMMUNICATION NAMES

MILITARY MEANING	NAVAJO PRONUNCIATION	NAVAJO MEANING
Telephone	Besh-hal-ne-ih	Telephone
Switchboard	Ya-ih-e-tih-ih	Central
Wire	Besh-le-chee-ih	Copper
Telegraph	Beesh-le-chee-ih-beh-hane-ih	Comm by copper wire
Semaphore	Dah-na-a-tah-ih-beh-hane-ih	Flag Signals
Blinker	Coh-nil-kol-lih	Fire Blinder
Radio	Nil-chi-hal-ne-ih	Radio
Panels	Az-kad-be-ha-ne-ih	Carpet Signals

OFFICERS NAMES

MILITARY MEANING	NAVAJO PRONUNCIATION	NAVAJO MEANING
Officers	A-la-jih-na-zini	Headmen
Major General	So-na-kih	Two stars
Brigadier General	So-a-la-ih	One star
Colonel	Atash-besh-le-gai	Silver Eagle
Lt.Colonel	Che-chil-be-tah-besh-legal	Silver Oak Leaf
Major	Che-chil-be-tah-ola	Gold Oak Leaf
Captain	Besh-legai-na-kih	Two Silver Bars
1st Lieutenant	Besh-legai-a-lah-ih	One Silver Bar
2d Lieutenant	Ola-alah-ih-ni-ahi	One Gold Bar

AIRPLANE NAMES

MILITARY MEANING	NAVAJO PRONUNCIATION	NAVAJO MEANING
Airplanes	Wo-tah-de-ne-ih	Air Force
Dive Bomber	Gini	Chicken Hawk
Torpedo Plane	Tas-chizzle	Swallow
Observation Plane	Ne-as-jah	Owl
Fighter Plane	Da-he-tih-hi	Humming Bird
Bomber	Jay-sho	Buzzard
Patrol Plane	Go-gih	Crow
Transport Plane	Atash	Eagle

SHIPS NAMES

MILITARY MEANING	NAVAJO PRONUNCIATION	NAVAJO MEANING
Ships	Toh-dineh-ih	Sea Force
Battleship	Lo-tso	Whale
Aircraft Carrier	Tsidi-ney-ye-hi	Bird Carrier
Submarine	Besh-lo	Iron Fish

-2-

The Code Talkers sent secret messages by phone and radio. Soldiers in Japan could not understand the code. The Code Talkers helped the United States win the war.

Do you have a password for your computer? A password is like a code. It lets you get in. It keeps other people out. It helps keep you and your messages safe.